Simply Inspired

...by sea glass
 & nature's gifts

Reflections, thoughts, and images
to enrich everyday living.

Linda Frothingham

This book is dedicated to my sister Barbara.

© 2016 Linda Frothingham

All rights reserved.

No part of this book may be reproduced in any written, electronic, recording, or photocopying form without the written permission of the publisher.

Books may be purchased in quantity by
contacting the publisher directly at
orders@peanucklepress.com

Photography: Linda Frothingham, Barbara Brooks, and Michael Frothingham Design: Frothideas.com

Peanuckle Press
Wilmette, IL 60091

ISBN: 978-1-944365-00-4 (Pbook)
ISBN: 978-1-944365-01-1 (Journal)
ISBN: 978-1-944365-02-8 (Ebook)

Library of Congress Control Number: 2015956052

1. Inspiration 2. Self-Help 3. Photography 4. Poetry

First Edition. Printed in the United States.

Simplyinspiredbook.com

To new beginnings
filled with inspiration
& motivation.

Envision a new awareness
of gifts of nature.

Be stirred by
meaningfulness in your
day-to-day life.

Let this be the start
to being
simply inspired.

Contents

Introduction 1

Sea glass, see the world 2

Nature clears the mind 4

An artist's view 6

Let the sunshine in 8

Testing the water 10

In the grand scene of things 12

Downstream 14

Let your imagination take you 16

With open eyes 18

The beach be with you 20

The bird's nest 22

New destiny 24

In flight 26

Be inspired by life 28

Quiet moments 30

Be on your way 32

Colorful sunset 34

Search of hearts 36

Deeper than mud	38
A good morning	40
Power of influence	42
Earth has it made	44
Our children learn from us	46
With me forever	48
What makes a paradise?	50
Tree house	52
Fresh water	54
Gift of friendship	56
Country stream	58
The closer look	60
Silhouettes	62
Fog sets in	64
Field of dreams	66
Give gratitude	68
The many seasons	70
The flowing river of energy	72
Find your gift	74
Ready for spring?	76
Be grounded	78
Just dandy	80

Choose your way	82
Seagulls ahead	84
So simple	86
Roam free	88
The night	90
Be it wild	92
Breaktime	94
Along the lake	96
Special places to remember	98
The light comes on	100
Let it shine	102
Find your passion	104
The vista	106
It guides you	108
Serenity here	110
Into the woods	112
Pursue your dreams	114
Red cardinal	116
To great endings	118
Thank you	120
About the author	121
Index	122-123

Introduction

Simply inspired.

This book began by a walk on the beach and the discovery of colorful sea glass at my fingertips – followed by discussion and appreciation of something so simple, yet filled with enlightenment. An 11-day cross-country hiking trip with my son brought nature back into my vision with a rekindled appreciation. A close encounter with a prairie rattlesnake made me grateful to be alive.

In celebration of life, I write this book.

This book is meant to be an inspiration for you to walk on the beach, get outside, play with your kids/grandkids, enjoy your friends, see the world and live life to the fullest. Images were taken from high up on a mountaintop in Montana to a country road in Pennsylvania, from across the world to Belize and in my backyard.

With thanks to Mother Nature, I write this book.

May these reflections and images inspire you each and every day.

Sea glass, see the world

It is early morning.
The sun a pink glow.
My toes touching the sand.
A cool breeze at my back as I walk.

There is not much time
for a quiet moment.
Not many are on the beach.
Not yet.

A smooth soft piece of sea glass draws my eye.
It's a shade of water, aqua blue.
Then another.
Pure frosted white glass.

I stop to reach for one.
Between my fingers, I smooth the sand away.
It's a gem in my fingertips.
I slip it in my pocket.

Sea glass.
See life in a new light. Will you?
I continue on my journey.
But much more slowly.

Go to the beach today.

And maybe you'll find sea glass.

Let the journey begin.

Nature clears the mind

Reach out to nature
for thoughts of grandeur.
Ideas will start to come.

Find a natural place to sit and be still.
Close your eyes.
Let your mind rest.

Make a wish list for life.
Keep it visible.
Share with a friend.

Find a way to make changes
for the better.
Work to keep the world safe.

It's in your hands, more than you know.
If you truly want it,
nothing will stop you.

Sit on the dock.

Set back the clock.

Find tranquility.

An artist's view

Been given a gift.
A brush in hand. Eyes wide open.
Artistry in full view for you to visit.

Can you see how Vincent Van Gogh saw the
spiraling, flame-like foliage of the cypress tree?
It was there all along. How did I miss it?

The tree leaves swirl in the wind.
Look up and ponder their existence.
The trees gently sway in unison.

See the world from the eyes of an artist.
The details stand out across the hillside.
The shapes of things turn into excitement.

Explore the beauty of nature inspiring.
Look closely at the drops of rain.
The wet blades of grass.

Examine colors in a pile of fall leaves.
Yellow ochre, deep purple, rich oranges.
A medley of natural earth tones.

The colors so delicate and alive.
See the world in a new light.
From an artist's vision.

Stop in my steps.

Look long at the
 many textures.

Notice nature in your life.

Let the sunshine in

Will a cloudy day bring you down?
A gray sky.
A wet walkway.
Little drops of rain on a bed of flowers.

Let positive prevail.
Let goodness be.
Encourage your mind
to be inspired.

Exercise your muscles,
inside and out.
Be brave. Reach out.
Help others.

Let the universe give gifts.
Sunshine is in your heart.
It's in your body.
It surrounds you.

Be strong and let emotions flow.
Experience the storms in life.
There is light at the end of the tunnel.
But you have to get there.

Make it the best it can be.

Stop to smell the roses.

Life is too short.

Seek a deeper meaning.

Testing the water

Do drop in.
Put your feet in the water.
It is cold.
Too cold.

Dip in again.
It is less chilling.
A third time.
It's like bath water.

Was it that way all along?
Or was it my reluctance?
It's hard to take that first step.
We must build courage.

If we jump in feet first
will it always be uncomfortable?
Do we know? Test the water.
Is that the building of confidence?

Or is it the fear of something new?
Like the first day of school.
A new job.
The adrenaline of life.

Let it take you away.

So inviting.

It is calming.

Be part of it.

In the grand scene of things

The days before the cell phone.
Our heads are filled with memories.
But only if we see things with our own eyes.
Really see things.

No distractions, please.
Not yesterday. Please, not today.
Oh, how I remember the day that I sat for hours.
High on top of the hill.

A rich blue sky.
Birds flying high.
A butterfly goes by.
See it so clearly.

The red barn in the distance.
Breaking the silence,
the sound of an ambulance
blaring over the hillside.

My mind races.
Is someone hurt? Was there an accident?
And then it is gone.
Silence once again.

Take a walk.

No need to talk.

Just listen.

The sounds of nature surround.

Downstream

The water rushes along
in the country creek.
So fast, yet in control.

A leaf drops from above.
It spins and swirls in the fast moving water,
sometimes getting hung up along the way.

Branches fallen across the creek.
Minnows move about it.
Tadpoles circle near the sides.

The area widens, eroding the hillside.
Changes are happening.
Fish dance, wiggle and sail.

Like in life, heading downstream.
Around the many places
where the path may get rocky.

Momentum picks up.
The leaf is released and on its way.
Freedom at last.

Under the surface.

Big trout. Little trout.

Catch them if you can.

Let your imagination take you

Two bikes parked.
They catch my eye.
Out in the middle of nowhere.

My mind wanders.
What is their story?
Are the riders coming back?

No locks on the bikes.
Oh, the level of trust.
Everything is quiet.

The bikes are waiting.
Time stops.
I want to know more.

Is it a young couple on a walk in the woods?
Or perhaps two boys that stopped to fish
in the nearby river?

I may never know the answer.
So I make up my own.
Where do the bikes take you?

Ready, set, go.

Think up a story.

Explore the world.

With open eyes

The day begins.
Whether driving, taking a train,
walking to work or play.
Go a new route.

Be on the lookout
for something new.
Like it's the first time you're seeing a place,
even if it's the 100th.

Watch for movement.
A puddle of water with raindrops.
Subtle nuances not to be missed.
Magical rays of light.

Take your time.
Look around.
Clear your thinking for this new day.
A new way. What do you say?

Stop and let stillness be.
Your senses will come alive.
Take in the view.
See it all new.

Take a new route.

Go in a new direction.

Be excited by it.

The beach be with you

The high grasses.
A pathway to the water.
Horseshoe crabs, after the big storm.

Oh, how I loved to go to the beach as a child.
An ocean of memories.
Fishermen line the wharf.

Teens enjoy the surf.
The building of sand castles.
A relaxing day.

Sand so white.
A breeze at my back.
Sailboats along the horizon.

The scent of the ocean.
Crash of the waves.
A sound so peaceful and yet so alive.

The water reveals the shells.
The many treasures along the way.
A piece of beach glass stands out.

Broken glass turns to beauty.
A gift to heal the heart.
Truly a treasure found.

Walk this way.

Refresh.

Relax.

Be at the beach.

The bird's nest

Have you ever watched a bird's nest being built?
It is a beautiful little construction job.
A work of art.

Discover a robin's egg in the nest.
The next day, another.
Sky blue eggs. So perfect.

Perched in a tree, for just me to see.
Shhhh. Don't get too close.
The mother keeps them warm with her underbelly.

New life cracks the shell.
The baby birds arrive.
Their skin so thin you can see their little veins.

So trusting and hungry.
Their mouths open wide to the sky.
Soft feathers magically appear.

The baby birds try to fly.
It takes a few tries,
but before you know it, they take flight.

Will you?

Robin's egg blue.

It is the little things
　　in life to notice.

Nature's beauty.

New destiny

A new destiny is near.
Just down the road.
To the many places
in the itinerary of life.

Find a way.
Be open to opportunities.
Turn a new corner.
How about today?

Step out of your comfort zone.
Be on the road ahead.
Let it lead you to newness.
Without second thoughts.

A place out of the ordinary.
Find the way to a path that
you would not normally cross.
Or to a city not on the map.

Down a winding road
that you may not know.
Be in the moment and away from the normal.
If not today, then how about tomorrow?

Journey ahead.

    The horse knows
        the way.

Find your way.

In flight

Birds in flight.
A lineup of geese
migrating across the blue sky.

Watch them closely.
See how they work in unison together.
The V formation is for victory.

Hear them honk a word of encouragement?
The V builds, as they cross the colorful skies.
Passing through the orange to blue.

Rotation of the leader that tires.
Giving each other the lift they need.
That is leadership. Perhaps friendship.

Flying together is so much better.
Take flight.
Friends through life.

Help each other reach higher,
go further, be better.
Share in the delight.

Precious moments.

Share them.

Find a bright spot today.

Be inspired by life

What will be your path in life?
Examine the steps to take.
Let emotions stir your thoughts.

Take control.
Be yourself.
Let things you love guide your way.

So many words of wisdom
we learn along the way.
What resonates with you?

Let thoughts form.
Ask questions?
Allow the answers to come.

What excites you?
What makes you smile?
What keeps you awake?

It is meditation in a way.
Look for the right direction
to find what truly inspires you.

Let the pathway
  guide you.

You will get there.

Quiet moments

A spring rain.
Blue sky reflects in the water.
A cloud passes.
The moment takes us in.

Walk to the edge of a garden.
The colors whisper.
Beauty at your touch.
Bring it around.

Stand high on a hillside.
The view stops us in our steps.
Watch and listen.
The wind brushes the trees.

Travel down a single lane road.
A horse grazes in the pasture.
Birds sing softly.
Be open to the spirituality of life.

An eagle soars by. Take notice.
Birds bathe in a puddle.
Their wings take flight.
They go on their way.

The quiet moments stand still.

Reflect on life.

May the sky
 guide your eyes.

Let your mind clear.

Be on your way

An early morning.
The silence is here.
It stirs something inside.
Have you heard it before?

An engine starts.
A plane crosses the sky.
It's time to get up.
Are you ready for the day?

There are voices of laughter.
Children playing outside.
The motion of the day.
Do you step out, or stay?

Decisions are made every day.
Some things are habits.
Others out of need.
What is right for you?

The choices are in front of you.
Let us open the door.
Step out.
Wake up the day.

Morning often leads
to sunshine.

Be ready.

Colorful sunset

Everything is quiet.
Peacefulness surrounds.
Listen closely.
Watch silently.

An unexpected moment.
The sunset this day.
Intense color that makes you stop in your steps
and take it all in.

It catches you by surprise.
The sky, an exquisite view.
Purple, blue, pastel pink to pure white.
The colorful vista changes minute by minute.

Take the time to admire it.
Watch the full process of nature.
The colors like a rainbow of ice cream.
So beautiful and brilliant.

The sky darkens.
It intensifies as the sun sets.
Then the gifts of color are gone
until the next time.

Nothing more invigorating
than a run on the beach
at sunset.

Perhaps bring a friend.

Search of hearts

Set out to find a message.
Some clarity in the day.
Be on the lookout.
It's time to start.

Head down a path
with one focus.
Going to a favorite destination.
The beach to find treasures.

Out to find re-creation.
Maybe find answers.
Find a sign
that things will be okay.

Is there hope? Is there love?
What makes our world more meaningful?
Is it in the way we look at life?
We need a sign that love is here.

Notice the stone in the shape of a heart?
Then spot a heart-shaped leaf.
A single flower petal in a heart shape.
Followed by a cloud that looks like a heart.

Was it secretly guiding me all along?
Perhaps I made it to my destination.

Look up.

Is that a heart?

Find your own meaning in things.

Deeper than mud

Love.
Higher than the sky.
Deeper than mud.

In the eyes of a child.
Unconditional love.
It's more than you can imagine.

Never ending love.
From deep in your heart.
To the realms of the sky.

From parents to children.
A passing of confidence.
The security of love.

A connection forever.
They learn for the better.
Grounded for life.

Higher than a mountain.
A way to show love.
Our hearts are connected.

Be young and free.

Enjoy moments
with nature.

Skip to my lou.

A good morning

Morning is inspiration to me.
Is it for you?
Get ready.

There is something special
about the early morning hours.
Dew on the grass.

The air is fresher, as if darkness has cleaned it.
Light pure and simple.
The glimmer of sun given freely.

Notice the colors.
Transparent rays angle down
through the clouds.

Observe the way the light hits the buildings,
a garden, the water, or comes through the trees.
And the way it changes. Ever notice that?

Take your time.
Look around. Stand still.
Clear your mind for a new day.

Take a deep breath.
Overcome resistance.
Take it one step at a time.

A morning walk brings
 thoughts of spring.

Seasons be. Finally.

Power of influence

Expand your world.
Live. Learn. Experience life.
Then share it.

Step away from technology.
Be mentally sharp.
Connect with each other.

We have the best computer in our brains.
Use it. Take charge.
Think! Take breaks.

Take chances.
It does not mean for you to do something dangerous.
It means to be prepared for what you do.

The layers of emotion and experiences
make us more human with a richer existence.
The memories we build, we can share.

We pass on our self-confidence.
Be inspired by your everyday connections.
Make the future better.

Let the seeds of life
be shared.

Be inspired by growth.

Earth has it made

Let earth inspire.
Most appreciated by many artists,
writers and great thinkers.
And perhaps by you?

Try something you never tried before.
Pick up a brush.
Paint with no holds barred.
Be engaged, without restraint.

The world is our canvas.
Take it in.
Or simply draw on the beauty
with your eyes.

Perhaps lead the way with a camera.
Or maybe a magnifying glass.
A telescope.
Any way to help you see.

Be adventurous. Be aware.
Be excited about the moment.
Let the beauty of nature
expand your inner peace.

A touch of color
    catches my eye along
        the mountain trail.

Does it catch yours?

Our children
learn from us

What do you say when you see a rainbow?
Is it good luck?
Is there a pot of gold at the end?
What do we pass on, generation to generation?

More than we realize at the time.
From mannerisms to simply a smile.
Our children are watching.
And they should be.

If we do it for them, they will not learn.
If they do it over and over again, they grow.
Mistakes are important to make.
Growing mentally is the substance of life.

Holding a hand on all of the firsts.
Till they can step alone.
Is that what parenting is?
Mother, may I? Yes, you may.

Will they take the steps to do the right thing?
What can I pass on to my children?
Greater insights and inspiration.
And as they grow, we also learn from them.

Let life give you
 a double rainbow.

It is in reach.

With me forever

Love the vast views.
The silence.
Spots where you can see for miles.
To where hillsides roll on and on.

An ocean goes in and out.
Never-ending motion.
Let nature be.
And your mind free.

From up on a mountaintop.
To the top of the world.
The day slows as you walk along.
Discover new scenes along the way.

Drive down the country road.
The animals in the distance.
All is quiet. Serene.
At peace.

Sometimes it's good to be alone
with no distractions.
The time to think
and become inspired.

Sunday drive.

Pull over.

Take your time.

What makes a paradise?

Serenity?
Beauty.
Colorful vistas.
Tropical flowers.

Sunrises.
Sunsets.
Blue waters like none other in the world.
A gentle breeze.

A warm bubble bath.
A cool refreshing walk.
Flowers that make you smile.
A warm hug from a friend.

A place of relaxation.
Comfort.
Simplicity.
Back to serenity?

What is right for you?
Where is your paradise?
Can you make your own paradise anywhere?
Indeed.

Snow capped mountains
rich with wildflowers.

Simply paradise.

Tree house

As kids, we played in the old oak tree.
Put our feet up, and relaxed for free.
Up above the world so high.
It's like a diamond in the sky.

We climbed to the very top.
To free our mind.
We sat high up on a branch.
From up above, we looked around.

The sounds and movement slowed.
Our eyes opened to the newness that surrounded.
Just reading a book.
Enjoying a simple time to relax.

We camped in the apple tree.
Crunched it for lunch.
Then up into the cherry tree.
We spit seeds below, as if we owned our world!

Our tree house was made
by using our imaginations.
Look up. Look out.
Grow with the branches of life.

Open up your mind.
   Nature is all around us.

Let inspiration grow.

Fresh water

It is all over the world.
But, do we appreciate it?
Water here.
So crystal clear.

The mountain stream.
A glistening lake. The vast ocean.
Fresh rain.
Mist in the air.

Taken for granted.
These basics in nature.
Water represents life.
Let it live.

From sea to shining sea.
Try not to waste a drop.
Give thoughts to saving it.
Our precious gold.

We are losing it.
What can you do about it?
Take care of our earth.
One person at a time.

Step this way.

It is waiting.

Experience the vista.

Gift of friendship

Good friends.
It is sharing and caring.
The moments to appreciate.
Gratitude in life.

Where are you today?
Do you have a hand to hold?
A shoulder to cry on?
A friend to take a walk with?

Be grateful for relationships.
Plant the seeds today.
Make an effort to give
the gift of friendship.

Start with taking action.
Reach out to a friend.
Offer an ear.
Be there.

And in the end you will be viewed as special
by someone you befriended.
From the inside out, without a doubt.
As a true friend.

An open doorway
    often leads
        to discovery.

Be brave. Make friends.

Country stream

Go on.
Sit by the water.
Put your fingers in it.

It is so cold.
So clean.
Totally invigorating.

Calming sounds.
A world at peace.
Let the water flow.

Be authentic
in our hearts and in our minds.
Let life trickle down.

Bring good thoughts.
Contemplate the future.
Remember the past.

Appreciate what life has to offer.
Let the water flow
into a stream of consciousness.

Let nature
    refresh your day.

Let it flow.

The closer look

When I was a young teen
my grandma lived on our farm.
She was not very old, but she had a bad heart.

She could look out the window and watch the birds.
Taking a simple walk was not an option.
So I would take pictures of things to share with her.

My eyes and discoveries became hers.
She was lucky. I was luckier.
For becoming aware and learning to care.

If I had not stopped to take a closer look,
I would not have had the chance
to give the gifts of nature to her.

From layered wet leaves
along a dirt path in the woods,
to a spring wildflower on top of the hill.

Fresh water springs reflect the blue sky.
Ice crystals form on a broken barn window.
One special moment at a time.

Shared then and now.
To my grandma with the big heart.
And now to you.

A pure country setting
with century-old
farm stones.

Time stands still.

Silhouettes

Silhouettes in life.
The black solid shapes stand out at dusk
against the drama in the sky.

When the sun sets
the contrast of light and dark accentuates.
The orange, yellows merge into the horizon.

The calm of the sun setting.
It's a relaxing feeling that takes over.
Be open to the emotion.

Watch for the black silhouette.
A fishermen on a dock.
Someone walking a dog on the beach.

Slow...slow...slow,
so slowly the sun descends.
It is there, and then it's gone.

A quiet beautiful view.
Each unique and never alike.
Almost magically it vanishes.

The masterpiece.
With its distinct shapes.
It turns into darkness.

The perfect place.

At the right time.

Smooth sailing.

Fog sets in

Like in life.
Some days you can't see in front of your own eyes.
Lost in the dampness.

Peacefulness is in the change.
The fog sets in.
Buildings disappear into the mist.

Look around.
Slow your mind. Calmly watch.
There is stillness.

The rain falls softly on your face.
A cool breeze on your back.
The colors change.

The trees go from green to shades of gray.
Our world is smaller.
No distance in sight.

It's a simple pleasure when the skies clear.
Bringing you clarity in your world
and in your life.

Nature comes
 and nature goes.

Life continues.

Field of dreams

Where do you get your inspiration?
Can you find it in your heart?
Be open. Nature is around us.

There's always a little something to observe.
Be it a nugget of sunshine in your window.
Or newly sprouting flowers in a garden.

Life offers us an open door.
Reach for it, before it is gone.
See what you might have missed.

In the eyes of children, all is new.
Should we take a lesson from a child,
examining every little gem of life?

Don't let life pass you by.
Look at the soft colors of a rainbow.
The perfect harmony in a leaf.

Look for subtle movements and special things.
A wind blown leaf.
A smooth stone on the beach.

Perhaps a butterfly stops just for you.
No matter your age, find your field of dreams
within a field of awareness.

Simply observe
 nature at work.

Beautiful.

Give gratitude

A new day.
What is in my way?
Is it time for accomplishments?
Promises to be fulfilled.

Music to be played.
Whatever artist I say?
Acts of kindness.
Any which way.

Go forth with a human connection.
Kind words to a friend.
A smile to a stranger.
Gratitude in many ways.

We can give a gift of warmth.
Some sunshine from our heart.
A sign that life is here to stay.
Give gratitude your way.

Be here in the moment.
And thankful for your world.
It is a new day.
The place to stay.

Sea art.

Share art.

Not sure? Just start.

Art inspires.

The many seasons

Seasons help count the years.
Some bring tears. Maybe fears.
It is going too fast.

Laughter echoes in the hearts of our childhood.
We built memories and feelings.
They blend the past with the future.

Let us start the day.
Bring us to a better place.
Enjoy the cycle of life.

The seasons change, and so do I.
From spring to summer.
Fall to winter. We grow.

Activities repeat
with growth to follow.
Change happens.

Sometimes good, sometimes sad.
Refreshing as a morning rain.
Or a new dusting of snow.

To a fresh new look around.
All evolving with change.
Through the many seasons. Are you ready?

Time stops
 when you let it.

Picture perfect.

The flowing river of energy

Go to a place that gives something in return.
A place to revitalize.
A great destination on the other side of the world.
Or a few miles away.

Find an opportunity to grow.
A time to be welcome.
Find the river of energy in your life.
Take hold.

Nature will help.
Let it take your breath away.
There are places in the world
ready for you to see.

Come discover. Walk.
Take the steps you always wanted to take.
Go to a place you have dreamed about.
A special spot to find balance in life.

Take on what you dream of doing.
Find a way to make it happen.
Aim all of your energy to the one goal.
Let the river of life flow passion.

Balancing life.

It starts with your mind, body and spirit.

Find healing.

Find your gift

What do you have to offer?
Kind words.
A gift of thought.
A moment of time.

Bring something special.
A batch of muffins.
A little plant for a friend.
Send a homemade card.

A single flower can start the healing.
Let life inspire you to blossom.
Then share that wealth.
Be proud of who you are.

Give a gift of caring.
Sharing.
Empathy in a special way.
Be a friend.

One heart to another heart.
An early morning call.
A welcome gift. Perhaps a piece of sea glass.
What better message can you send?

Petals so fresh.

      Colors so soft.

A gift.

Ready for spring?

Winter ice.
It does entice.
White clouds above the earth.

The spark of color appreciated.
When all is mainly white.
It's a pretty sight.

Winter clears the air.
The chill kills the germs.
The cold chills the bones.

Then it's finally over.
You're ready to get back outside.
Go forth.

Do you see the colors?
Some hidden.
Others out in the open.

The buds come out.
Daffodils bloom.
Tulips burst with color.

Open your eyes.
And find the signs.
Are you ready for spring?

Look around for
    a sign of spring.

It's just the start.

Be grounded

Nature is your friend.
Birds and sounds can keep you company.
And give you the comfort you sometimes need.

Let the wind push you to new destinies.
Be ready for the ups and downs.
Keep balanced and be in control.

Be a leader in your own way.
When your heart says, "No," listen to it.
Trust your gut.

When in your heart it feels right, go with it.
Calm the internal whispers of doubt.
Let nature and your conscience guide you.

Am I good enough to compete in my dreams?
Will I make it to the water? Or to a mountain?
What will fate bring to me?

Let nature be your friend.
Guide you in your thoughts
and be at your side. Just focus.

Every day can move you forward
toward success in all aspect of your life.
Let it be.

Nurture nature
 on a quiet road.

Let the view lift you.

Just dandy

The dandelion.
So bright and yellow.
Along the highway.

A mass of yellow.
If it is pretty to you
who really cares if it's just growing wild?

Take a closer look.
It changes like magic.
And ends with a wish.

As a child my job was to fill baskets
with hundreds of little yellow flowers.
My grandfather made sweet dandelion wine.

I treasure the moment.
Dandelions bring back memories.
That is a gift in itself.

Some people see them as a weed.
Others see them
as something very special.

Is it a wish or a weed?

It's all in how
      you see it.

It is always a wish.

Choose your way

Where do you choose to go?
Where do you choose to be?
What is it going to take to get there?

All roads lead to somewhere.
Plan a journey for you.
A lifetime of experience.

How will you get there?
What is your way?
Be inspired by your insights.

Let the things you really love take you there.
Follow your interests.
Let them guide you.

Get where you want to go.
There is a way.
It's waiting.

You choose to make it happen.
Step forward, not back.
Choose your own way.

Alive with energy,
    yet calming
        and tranquil.

Reach it.

Seagulls ahead

On the beach.
A seagull lands ahead.
The waves drift in slowly.

A shimmering wetness invigorates, yet calms.
Your mind clears.
Stop and watch.

Let the worries of life take a break.
Let stillness be.
The texture of the sand goes from smooth to rough.

Peacefulness surrounds.
It is easy to take a relaxing deep breath now.
And let go.

Nature gives this to you.
A rewarding point in time.
Appreciate the moment.

A serenity that matches life.
Relax and let it flow.
My steps are slower now.

Take the time to look around.
Watch the seagull fly away.
Can we spare the time?

What are they
 waiting for?

Perhaps you.

So simple

There are times in your life
that make you want to stand still.
With no agenda.
No rush to get anywhere.

Simplicity is life.
At least it could be.
Doing everything twenty-four/seven
is not always a good thing.

Was it that way in the good old days?
We think our lives are more complicated now.
But maybe not so.
We just need to step back.

See the seat in front of you.
Get on it now
and let your feet hang free.
Let your hair blow in the wind.

Let the swing fly up
and out, and back.
Be free as a kid again.
Take that journey.

The swing
 waits for you.

Get on.

Roam free

It is a beautiful day.
Driving through the mountains.
The view is better around every bend.
Regarded now with open eyes.

The greens are rich from the spring waters.
The snow on the mountaintops -
a beauty to behold.
Bluish gray mountains stand out with perfection.

Weave along the winding road.
Notice movement.
In the distance, a huge elk in the field.
It enters the water.

So picturesque, pull over.
Stop and watch.
The elk works its way slowly across the river.
It enters the woods and an experience is sealed.

We shared the moment.
It brings you home.
A memory etched in my mind.
Forever.

Solitude can be
	very healing.

Be open.

The night

The glimmer of the lights
light up your life.
It can be the stars in the sky.
Or city lights that twinkle.

Be still and take it in with a glimmer of hope.
The earth stands still for you.
Don't let the city sounds disrupt.
And disturb your view of the night.

See the special things that catch your eyes.
Watch for the movement of a firefly.
Surround yourself with the power of passion.
A streetlight glows just for you.

A faint candlelight shines on.
Look at life from different angles.
Observe every inch of the world.
Bring it to life.

A calm night sky.
Open your eyes.
Let the incredible scenes
glimmer in your mind.

City lights
   come alive.

See the world from a new view.

Be it wild

Treasure the abundance
in the offerings of nature.
Be on the lookout for rewards.
The blueberries are ripe and ready to eat!

Is that a morel mushroom?
A gift near the old elm down.
Awaken to what is here.
The many gifts in the wild.

As kids, we would sit in the field of clover.
We would hunt for hours in the mass of three leaves.
On occasion, find a four-leaf clover!
And luck would be our reward.

And there it is.
The abundance of mint.
It is a gift of tea for me.
It grows wild in our garden.

A favorite in our neighborhood.
Raspberries. Growing year to year.
You can eat as many as you pick.
Find even more. Spread jam for all.

A successful
 treasure hunt
 of morels.

Treasures to find.

Breaktime

We get so wrapped up in life that
sometimes we just need a break.
No one seems to have time to relax and have fun.
You have to make time.

If you live near a beach, get to it.
Walk barefoot.
If you've never sailed, sign up.
Ever go where no man has gone before?

Life is about going for it.
Just do it. Find a way. Walk for miles.
If you don't do the things you want to do
you may never get to them.

If you live near a mountain,
make sure you climb it to the top.
Is there a creek you can cross?
Find one. Sit by the side.

Study a map with an eye for adventure.
Be ready to explore.
See the world from a new perspective.
If not today, then when?

Summer is waiting.

All you need is the time.

All breaks inspire.

Along the lake

Why do people flock to the beaches?
It takes you and everyone
into a state of being.

To the home of tranquility.
It is a calm that settles the nerves.
A place with no stress.

The rocks on your feet
are like a massage.
They soften as you experience them.

And then there is the white sand.
Step in it with your bare feet.
Dip into the water with your toes.

We invite you to the lake
for peacefulness.
Calmness.

Quietness.
And stillness.
Whatever is right for you.

An early morning walk.

Find gifts along the
edge of the water.

Step forward.

Special places to remember

There are places in our world
that make you want to go back.
You are drawn in.

What makes them stand out?
Was it the way you felt?
Or was it the person you were with?

Memories are meant to be treasured.
Where is it for you?
Have you been there yet?

A picture brings you back.
It is like going home.
In your mind or captured in a frame.

Should you keep seeing new places?
There are so many places to discover.
Where to for you?

Can you fit it in?
You sure can try. Start today.
Find sanctuary in your life.

Be appreciative
 of the sanctuary.

A special place to be.

The light comes on

We are open for inspiration.
An opportunity to reach out.
To stand proud of who we are.
There is a way.

We have this day before us.
A lifetime to work with.
It can start with something simple.
And inspire along the way.

Drop a penny
so others can find it.
Put sea shells on the beach
for children to discover.

Silently help others.
Give rather than take.
Without wanting something in return.
Only internal satisfaction.

Do some good in our day-to-day lives.
We can do so much more than we know.
It is our chance to shine.
What is in your plan?

Dusk to twilight
 on a summer's night.

Sit for it.

Let it shine

The sun.

A sense of energy.

A warm touch of security.

Seal your lips and open your mind.

Let the warmth enrich your world.

Take the time to absorb.

Be in a place that excites you.

Relax and explore your feelings.

Connect to your inner self.

Let your thoughts wander.

See where they go.

Be open.

This poem was written when I was 19.

Be in the moment.

Wait patiently.

Be mesmerized.

Find your passion

Simplicity.
Find your passion within it.
The orchid.
The design compels the inner soul.

It is pure and refined.
With unparalleled elegance.
An orchid blooms.
It waits so patiently for all to see.

It feeds the spirit with its stillness.
A prolonged beauty.
Stay still and be rewarded.
It is simply enchanting.

Oh, the exquisite orchid.
From the start it calms the heart.
It keeps you company.
It pushes the passing of time for lonely hearts.

It will last.
It's a treasure of pride and joy.
Turn to the window.
Let sunshine in.

Refinement
   from an exotic place.

Delicate beauty.

The vista

Step into the world of beauty.
A cause for adventure.
Let details grab you.
Stop you on a walk.

A view to simply appreciate.
The soft textures.
The native grasses.
The subtle colors in the natural environment.

Today I walked for hours.
Enjoying the pure freedom, the peace of mind.
See the many prairie dogs, snakes and buffalo?
Yes, to all.

Preserved for future generations.
Be alert to the possibilities.
Let it set you free.
The journey. Be part of it.

The day starts with
a cool breeze.

And ends with a
warm heart.

Stop and take it all in.

It guides you

Give yourself the time.
Go explore.
Reunite.
Be guided by nature.

Get to a place you love.
To one of the great wonders
of the world.
Or to a place you can relate.

Search for beauty.
Place it at your fingertips.
Take nature in.
Rediscover your inner self.

A chance to take it slower.
The time to breathe in the mountain air.
A quiet mind. Without a care.
Just be there.

Awaken the clarity.
Get to the place that feels right.
Find joy in your life.
Have you found it yet?

Some places on earth
are simply out
of this world.

See them.

Serenity here

We walk across a field.
White snow for miles.
The peacefulness simply
relaxes our presence.

The sky blends softly into the snow.
No movement.
The earth stands still.
A chill you feel.

The trees barely move.
Farm equipment at a standstill.
A bird flies out of a tree.
Then stillness again.

Be calmed by the beauty in nature.
The serenity that is around us.
It takes you to a place of transformation.
Be present and share the love of life.

Let it stand still.

And it does.

In silence.

Into the woods

Walking hand in hand through the woods.
No destiny in mind.
Enjoying nature, one place at a time.

As we journey through life
we travel to places so near and so far.
Do we really see the beauty?

From here to there.
Like what we have, not what we want.
Balance the give and take of life.

If you could climb any mountain, where would it be?
If you could walk any path, where would it lead?
If you went around the world, where would you stop?

Sometimes it's the places
that are the closest that we miss.
Everything you need might just be there.

Open your eyes.
Notice things.
Start by simply looking around.

Bees pollinate flowers.

Enough said?

Be thankful for nature.

Pursue your dreams

May the morning awaken your spirit.
Spark your emotion inside.
Expand your full being.

Realize your personal potential.
Feel good about what you are accomplishing.
What you are doing this special day.

What if you had an extra hour just for you?
Ten minutes to close your eyes,
reflect on the day.

Make time to have your morning coffee.
Relax, even if just for a moment.
A precious moment.

Let this be the day you decide to wake up early.
Be truly happy to start this day.
To pursue your dreams.

Be it a sweet gesture.
A major accomplishment in life.
It's up to you. Go and do it.

Cock-a-doodle-do.

Wake up
one and all.

To the morning.

Red cardinal

Red cardinal in motion.
Chirps to get my attention.
Very special in my eyes' view.

A bright bird standing out so beautifully.
Perched above glimmering winter snow.
Or against summer shades of green.

Red cardinal flies nearby.
Saying, "Hi."
For a moment, time stops.

A message of love.
Sent by my red courier.
I hope. Believing it is a sign of love.

A visitor from far away.
Here at my window.
From my gone, but not forgotten, dear Dad.

The red male cardinal flies away.
My heart softens.
With love I look up in the sky.

My father's
    wooden red cardinal
        in my backyard.

A gift of love.

To great endings

When life become too much, what then?
How do we keep going?
Overcoming obstacles
driving us to quit?

What is the secret to satisfaction?
Financial? Relationships?
Finding inner peace?
We try. We fail.

Think it through.
Question every decision.
Evolve.
Where is the rainbow?

Reach out to friends, to family.
Maybe to strangers.
Try with all of our heart to find the answers.
Is it that we simply don't give up?

And finally, when we have tried everything,
when we are about to say, "I give,"
set forth a new plan.
To inspire...and be simply inspired.

Open up your heart.

Remember those
 you care about.

Love continues in our hearts.

Thank you

Life is special.
Friends are special.
My family is special.

My husband, John, and my children, Kathryn and Michael, have always been appreciative and supportive of my life as an artist, a "creative." From my writing, drawing and painting, to my silly playing. They laugh with me and smile at me. My wonderful son-in-law, Mike, follows in my footsteps of marketing.

And to my friends that stand by me. Anne, Barbara, Chris, Debbie, Jen, Laurie, Mary, Meg, Meghanne, Matt, Philippa, Sue, and Vero. Thank you.

All photos are by Linda Frothingham
unless credited here:

Pages 63, 67, 83, 85, 97 photos by Barbara Brooks.
Pages 51, 77, 89 photos by Michael Frothingham.

About the author

Linda Frothingham is an experienced "creative" professional. She worked for the world's top advertising agencies, Ketchum PR, and J. Walter Thompson, which led to starting her own successful Chicago marketing firm.

Linda's passion is storytelling. She is also a professional artist. Her interests are writing, photography, travel, sports and hiking.

She grew up on a farm in Pennsylvania and will forever hold the gift of nature and the outdoors in her heart. With this book she shares some of her insights and reflections on life.

Linda lives in Wilmette, Illinois, a short walking distance to the beach. Complete with sea glass.

Index of Poem titles (left sides)
& Photo reflections (right sides)

A good morning 40	Earth has it made 44
A morning walk brings 41	Field of dreams 66
A pure country setting 61	Find your gift 74
A successful treasure hunt 93	Find your passion 104
A touch of color 45	Fog sets in 64
Alive with energy 83	Fresh water 54
Along the lake 96	Gift of friendship 56
An artist's view 6	Give gratitude 68
An early morning walk 97	Go to the beach today 3
An open doorway 57	In flight 26
Art of nature 117	In the grand scene of things 12
Balancing life 73	Into the woods 112
Be appreciative 99	Introduction 1
Be grounded.....................78	Is it a wish or a weed? 81
Be in the moment 103	It guides you 108
Be inspired by life 28	Journey ahead 25
Be it wild 92	Just dandy 80
Be on your way 32	Let it shine 102
Be young and free 39	Let it stand still 111
Bees pollinate flowers 113	Let life give you 47
Breaktime 94	Let nature refresh your day.............59
Choose your way 82	Let the pathway guide you 29
City lights come alive 91	Let the seeds of life be shared 43
Cock-a-doodle-do 115	Let the sunshine in 8
Colorful sunset 34	Let your imagination take you 16
Country stream 58	Look around for a sign 77
Deeper than mud 38	Look up 37
Dig a deep hole 88	Morning often leads 33
Downstream 14	Nature clears the mind 4
Dusk to twilight 101	Nature comes and nature goes 65

New destiny 24	Step this way 55
Nothing more invigorating 35	Stop in my steps 7
Nurture nature 79	Stop to smell the roses 9
Open up your heart 119	Summer is waiting 95
Open up your mind 53	Sunday drive 49
Our children learn from us 46	Take a new route 19
Petals so fresh 75	Take a walk 13
Power of influence 42	Testing the water 10
Precious moments 27	The beach be with you 20
Pursue your dreams 114	The bird's nest 22
Quiet moments 30	The closer look 60
Ready for spring? 76	The day starts with a cool breeze 107
Ready, set, go 17	The flowing river of energy 72
Red cardinal 116	The light comes on 100
Refinement 105	The many seasons 70
Reflect on life 31	The night 90
Roam free 88	The perfect place 63
Robin's egg blue 23	The swing waits for you 87
Sea art 69	The vista 106
Sea glass, see the world 2	Time stops 71
Seagulls ahead 84	To great endings 118
Search of hearts 36	To new beginnings 2
Serenity here 110	Tree house 52
Silhouettes 62	Under the surface 15
Simply observe 67	Walk this way 21
Sit on the dock 5	What are they waiting for? 85
Snow capped mountains 51	What makes a paradise? 50
So inviting 11	With me forever 48
So simple 86	With open eyes 18
Solitude can be very healing 89	
Some places on earth 109	
Special places to remember 98	

Be simply inspired.

www.ingramcontent.com/pod-product-compliance
Lightning Source LLC
Chambersburg PA
CBHW040416100526
44588CB00022B/2843